Teaching Listening

Steven Brown

CAMBRIDGE UNIVERSITY PRESS

CAMBRIDGE UNIVERSITY PRESS
Cambridge, New York, Melbourne, Madrid, Cape Town, Singapore, São Paulo

Cambridge University Press
32 Avenue of the Americas, New York, NY 10013-2473, USA

www.cambridge.org

© Cambridge University Press 2006

This book is in copyright. Subject to statutory exception
and to the provisions of relevant collective licensing agreements,
no reproduction of any part may take place without
the written permission of Cambridge University Press.

First published 2006

Printed in the United States of America

Book layout services: Page Designs International

Table of Contents

Introduction   1

1   Activation of prior knowledge for improved listening comprehension   2

2   Systematic presentation of listening for main ideas, listening for details, and listening and making inferences   5

3   Stimulating integration of real-world cultural information for students to know and share   7

4   Presentation of extensive listening tasks leading to personalized speaking   9

References and Further Reading   11

Introduction

Two themes will wind through this discussion. The first is the necessity of supporting students' learning. Listening in another language is a hard job, but we can make it easier by applying what we know about activating prior knowledge, helping students organize their learning by thinking about their purposes for listening, and if speaking is also a goal of the classroom, using well-structured speaking tasks informed by research.

Another theme will be motivation. Because listening is so challenging, teachers need to think carefully about making our activities successful and our content interesting.

Both themes are united by a focus on the students. We need to capitalize on the knowledge and interests they already possess. Then we need to help them apply that knowledge and those interests so they can become effective listeners.

1 | *Activation of prior knowledge for improved listening comprehension*

One very important idea for teaching listening is that listening courses must make use of students' prior knowledge in order to improve listening comprehension. To make this idea clear, this section introduces several concepts from the cognitive view of language learning, including schema, scripts, and top-down/bottom-up processing. This section also considers the similarities and differences between listening and reading, and then looks specifically at why the activation of prior knowledge is perhaps even more important in listening than in reading comprehension. Finally, there is a concrete example of activating prior knowledge in listening materials.

We have known at least since the 1930s that people's prior knowledge has an effect on their cognition. Prior knowledge is organized in schemata (the plural form of schema): abstract, generalized mental representations of our experience that are available to help us understand new experiences. Another way to look at this phenomenon is the idea of scripts. For example, everyone who has been to a restaurant knows that there is a predictable sequence of questions involved in ordering a meal. In the United States these have to do with whether you want soup or salad, the kind of dressing on the salad, choice of side dishes, etc. Even if you do not hear a question, perhaps because the restaurant is too noisy, you can guess from your place in the script what the server is probably asking. Unfortunately, this script does not transfer perfectly from country to country because the routine is slightly different in each place. However, when traveling in another country, and eating in a restaurant, you can make certain assumptions about the kinds of questions that will be asked. If food has been ordered but drinks have not, and the server asks another question, you might fairly predict that the question is about the choice of drinks, based on your prior knowledge of what happens in restaurants. Indeed, successful language learners often can be separated from unsuccessful language learners by their ability to contextualize their guesses and use their prior knowledge in this way.

The idea of prior knowledge is one part of the cognitive model of language processing. That model says that when people listen or read, we process the information we hear both top-down and bottom-up. *Top-down* means using our prior knowledge and experiences; we know certain things about certain topics and situations and use that information to understand. *Bottom-up* processing means using the information we have about sounds, word meanings, and discourse markers like *first, then* and *after that* to assemble our understanding of what we read or hear one step at a time.

I like to use as an example of the two kinds of processing my experience buying postcards at an Austrian museum. I speak no German. Having calculated that the postcards would cost sixteen schillings, I walked up to the counter and gave the clerk a twenty-schilling note. She opened the cash register, looked in it, and said something in German. As a reflex, I dug in my pocket and produced a one-schilling coin and gave it to her. She smiled and handed me a five-schilling coin. I managed the conversation based on my prior knowledge of how one deals with small change at a store. In some sense, I didn't need to speak German, I just needed my prior knowledge. Later on that same trip, however, I did need to manage a transaction "bottom up" when I asked at the Madrid train station for tickets and was answered by a torrent of language that included the word *huelga* – Spanish for "strike." There had been a strike that morning. Here, my "getting tickets" script failed, and I needed words – just one in this case – to understand what was going on.

Reading courses have used the ideas of prior knowledge and top-down processing for years, typically in the form of pre-reading questions or tasks. The purpose of a pre-reading task is usually to activate students' prior knowledge. If the reading is about a famous person, for example, the task might require students to list as many things as they can about that person. Reading courses also have used the idea of bottom-up processing when they have pre-taught new vocabulary and other word- and sentence-level knowledge that students might need to know before reading.

Students obviously need both bottom-up and top-down processing skills in listening as well. Students must hear some sounds (bottom-up processing), hold them in their working memory long enough (a few seconds) to connect them to each other and then interpret what they've just heard before something new comes along. At the same time, listeners are using their background knowledge (top-down processing) to determine meaning with respect to prior knowledge and schemata.

The cognitive view of language learning sees listening comprehension as being basically the same as reading comprehension and consequently pedagogical practices have been very similar: In a typical lesson, there are "pre" activities, "while" activities, and "post" activities. However, teachers know that, despite our practice, listening is a bit different from reading. For instance, students can skim a text quickly to get a good idea what it's about, but listeners can't skim. The language comes rushing in at them. Listening must be done in real time; there is no second chance, unless, of course, the listener specifically asks for repetition. When students read, cognates (words that are similar in two languages) help understanding. But while cognates may look alike on the page, their sounds may be quite different and they may be less useful while listening. Listening also involves understanding all sorts of reductions of sounds and blending of words. There are false starts and hesitations to be dealt with. In a study that compared reading and listening in a foreign language (Lund 1991), it was found that readers recalled more details than listeners, and that listeners, while understanding a lot of the main ideas, had to "fill in the blanks" in their understanding by guessing at context. Again, with the words rushing in and the student having no control, these findings make sense.

At this point, there is a need to introduce one more concept from cognitive psychology: the human as a limited processor of information. Think of the ability to pat your head and rub your stomach at the same time. This is an interesting analogy to apply to listening because it is first a matter of individual differences: Some people can do this better than others. So it goes with listening. Some people are inherently better listeners than others. But even the best listeners, as anyone who has studied or taught a language knows, can have a difficult time. Like patting your head and rubbing your stomach, listening in a foreign language is subject to individual differences. Our task as teachers is to first understand that all humans are limited in their ability to process information. Then we must figure out a way to help, to take away some of the difficulty. That's where activating prior knowledge comes in.

In the context of a listening class, one could take the following approach. Let's assume the topic is jobs. The goal is to give students practice in listening for job titles. Even if students are not employed, they have spent a good part of their lives hearing about the jobs people do. They certainly know the names of many jobs in their first language. They may even know several common job titles in English (like *doctor* and *teacher*). They probably don't know how to say other jobs in English. A pre-listening task should have two parts, then. Students should have an opportunity to learn vocabulary items (and perhaps structures) they don't know but that they will need to successfully complete the task. However it is just as important to give the students the opportunity to use what they already know – their prior knowledge – to help them do the task. This may take the form of having them list jobs they know how to say in English. It really doesn't matter whether the words actually will appear in the listening task because activating prior knowledge, in addition to helping comprehension, motivates students by bringing their lives into the lesson.

In summary, listening is a complex activity, and we can help students comprehend what they hear by activating their prior knowledge. The next section will consider another way teachers can help ease the difficulty of listening: training students in different types of listening.

2 | Systematic presentation of listening for main ideas, listening for details, and listening and making inferences

We always have a purpose for listening. We may listen to the radio in the morning to decide whether to wear a coat or take an umbrella. We may listen to a song for pleasure. We listen in different ways based on our purpose. Having a purpose helps us listen more effectively. For example, when listening to a weather report, if our purpose is to decide whether to wear a coat, we want to focus on the temperature. In English, we listen with extra care to the end of the phrase that begins with ". . . highs in the . . ." which is routinely used to indicate the warmest temperature that we can expect for the day.

In the past, listening material was frequently based on a series of post-listening comprehension questions (*What times does the train leave? How much does the ticket cost?*). One of the reasons that approach to listening didn't serve students very well was that they generally had no idea of why they were listening until after the fact (unless the teacher gave them the questions beforehand, which many did not).

We can help students listen more effectively if we spend some time teaching them about purposes for listening. One way to do that is to use a simple dialogue like the one below in order to show how they might listen differently depending on their goals.

> Woman: We're going out to dinner after class. Do you want to come, too?
> Man: Maybe. Where are you going?
> Woman: Pizza King.
> Man: Pizza? I love pizza!

First of all, students could listen for the main idea. You might set this sort of task: "What's the most important idea in this conversation? What is the main thing they are talking about?" Write some choices on the board: *Class? Dinner?* After the listening, students would answer, "Dinner." Point out that to be successful, they didn't need to understand anything else. They just had to understand that "dinner" is the main idea of the conversation. Listening for main ideas means that the listener wants to get a general idea of what is being said. The details are less important.

There are other ways to listen, however. We sometimes need to listen for details. To point this out, use the same dialogue, but this time set this task: "What are they going to eat?" When students answer "Pizza" point out that to be successful, they needed only to understand one detail of the conversation: that the woman and her friends are going out for pizza, not hamburgers or spaghetti.

Listening for details is something we do every day. For example, we need the details when we are getting directions to someplace like a friend's home. Just understanding the topic in this case does us no good.

A third important reason for listening is listening and making inferences. Speakers do not always say exactly what they mean. That is, important aspects of meaning are sometimes implied rather than stated. Listeners have to "listen between the lines" to figure out what really is meant.

To get this point across, again use the pizza dialogue. This time ask, "Is the man going to go with them?" Point out that the man says that he loves pizza, so he probably will go. Sometimes people do not say exactly and directly what they mean. Students need practice in listening between the lines.

Systematically presenting (1) listening for main ideas, (2) listening for details, and (3) listening and making inferences helps students develop a sense of why they listen and which skill to use to listen better. Teachers can build skills by asking students to focus on their reason for listening each time they listen. This is a form of strategy training. Strategies are clearly a way to ease the burden of listening and should be taught. However, the problem with a lot of strategy training is that there are so many strategies. There are literally books full of them. One approach is to choose a select number of strategies and to teach them repeatedly. The idea of knowing the purpose of listening is a very effective first strategy to teach because it helps students organize and reflect on their learning. (Mally and Chamot, 1990).

If students know why they are listening, they are more focused. Think back to the statement that the human mind is limited in its ability to process information. Teachers can help students understand what they are hearing if we activate their prior knowledge, teach them (or remind them of) the words that are useful for the listening task, and tell them the purpose of their listening. All of these things lessen the considerable demands that listening comprehension makes on students. That's not the whole story of listening, of course. The next section will take up the crucial matters of culture and motivation.

3 *Stimulating integration of real-world cultural information for students to know and share*

Teaching students about something other than the language they are learning is a logical outcome of the idea of communicative language teaching (CLT) because one of the principles of CLT is the presentation and practice of meaningful language in a context. When we teach materials in a context, we move beyond language as a set of example sentences to language as it is situated in the world.

The primary place language is situated is in culture. Most students of a foreign language are interested in the culture of the places where the language they are studying is spoken. English presents an interesting case with regard to culture because it is now an international language. To cite only a few examples, English is used by clerks in North America, by university lecturers in India, and by businesspeople in Korea who use it to communicate with colleagues from elsewhere in Asia. Even in culturally homogeneous countries, students are eager to learn about the lives of others who speak English, including others who speak English as an additional language. Students today realize that they will be using English to communicate with people from all over the world.

One result of the widespread use of English is that there exists an information gap between many of its speakers. Students will naturally wish to share their own culture and learn about other cultures through the medium of English. This sharing of culture is potentially very motivating. It is motivating to hear about cultures you're unfamiliar with, and it is motivating to find the words to describe your own culture in English. Teachers know that keeping students' interest is key to learning, especially in classrooms where motivation can sometimes be a problem.

The base on which most motivational research has been done is the distinction between instrumental motivation and integrative motivation. With respect to language learning, instrumental motivation is the desire to pass a test or obtain a qualification while integrative motivation is the desire to be a part of the culture that speaks that language. Though largely unproven, the assumption in English language teaching has been that instrumental motivation is closely identified with EFL situations, while integrative motivation is closely tied to ESL situations. That may be true, but it reduces EFL teaching to the role of English-as-test-preparation (preparation for university entrance exams, for standardized exams like TOEIC, TOEFL, etc.). Dörnyei (2005) and others have expanded the definition of motivation, however, realizing that the instrumental/integrative dichotomy does not address all the issues we find in language learning.

Much of the current work on motivation places it in the context of the classroom in general rather than specifically in the EFL/ESL situation. The key is in that old cliché "Success breeds success." The conditions under which students work and the materials they use are important, as are students' continued positive approach to the class.

An important new idea in motivation is Dörnyei's (2005) notion of students constructing an "ideal L2 self." An ideal language self is essentially what one wants to be in the language; it is connected with hopes and looks toward growth, so it is connected to motivation. This is an important aspect of using culture as a topic in the classroom. First of all, it means that students do not have to integrate into anybody else's culture in order to be that ideal language self. They do not have to be American or British to speak English. They can keep their own cultures and still speak English, and they can share their native cultures in English.

One way to present culture effectively to beginning and intermediate students is to recycle topics from other lessons and expand those topics in a cultural context. The information in the following task was taken from an authentic interview; it provides a model of a competent English speaker from a country where English is a foreign language. The topic of food is recycled and expanded as the speaker compares popular dishes in Thailand with those in the United States.

> Woman: But you know, the pad Thai in the U.S. is not the same as in Thailand. In Thailand it's sweet like it is here, but it's also very spicy – much spicier than it is here in the U.S. That's the way I like it – the real Thai way.

Real-world, interesting cultural information teaches students something new. It also leads to increased motivation.

4 | *Presentation of extensive listening tasks leading to personalized speaking*

When we think of listening textbooks and classes, we have a tendency to think of students listening to a recording and doing a task. They overhear other people talk and then react to that conversation. This sort of task is important because it allows teachers to isolate student responses and thereby gauge the progress the students are making on listening skills. Courses that focus exclusively on listening skills can be quite effective, and some programs have a curriculum that necessitates a class devoted solely to listening. Other programs pair listening and speaking. That is also appropriate because much of the time when we use language naturally, we pair listening and speaking. We are sometimes the listener and sometimes the speaker. If time allows, it is natural in listening courses to give students a chance to practice listening to other students as well as to an audio recording. This means teachers may wish to have students spend some time speaking to each other.

For this reason, this section considers features of good speaking tasks. Much of the research done in second language acquisition through the years has focused on speaking. We know quite a bit about good speaking tasks, and some of the features of effective speaking tasks are described below. (See Ellis 2003 for a more complete summary).

Two-way speaking tasks, sometimes called jigsaw tasks, require students to share some information with others; these are popular in speaking classes. An example is a simple pair-work activity in which two people have different pictures and they must find the differences between the pictures. These tasks are popular because they engage the students and are fun. Researchers think they lead to language acquisition because they generally lead to more negotiation of meaning (questions or clarifications) than one-way tasks do. A one-way task involves one person explaining something to the rest of the class. For example, the teacher might describe a drawing and the students would have to replicate it. In general, there are fewer questions asked of the teacher, in this case, than of the pair-work partner. Negotiation of meaning, in which students have to come to a shared understanding, has been seen as one of the engines that drives language learning.

Closed tasks, which have only one acceptable outcome or answer, lead to more negotiation than open tasks, for which there is more than one acceptable outcome. In an activity that requires students to find the differences in two pictures, there will be an exact number of differences – let's say eight. To complete the task, to reach closure, students need to find all eight. In contrast an open task like "Tell your partner what you did this weekend" leads to less negotiation because there is little need for both partners to agree on an understanding. If one doesn't understand but doesn't want to embarrass the partner by asking questions, the task goes on, and its completion is not affected in any way. On the other hand, if the task were closed so that the pair would have to find three things they both did that weekend, the negotiation would increase because of the need to come to an agreement.

Good speaking tasks often have an element of pre-task planning. One of the recurring problems with the communicative approach to language teaching has been that teachers sometimes do not fully prepare students for the tasks they will be doing. There is now a line of research in language teaching (Ellis 2005) that shows how taking a small amount of time (as little as one or two minutes) to plan what will be said during the task can pay large dividends in terms of accuracy, fluency, and complexity of language produced. This might not surprise some teachers, but others are used to putting their students directly into tasks because they've been told that teacher talk is bad, and that students should be doing the talking. That's somewhat true, but preparing students does not have to take the form of lecture. Giving students a minute or two, alone or with a partner, to think about what they will say (after the teacher has given the instructions for the activity) generally leads to students producing more accurate sentences, longer turns of conversation, and more complex language.

Teachers often see the course as moving through the textbook, completing one activity, and then moving on to the next. However, doing the same or similar activities over again can be a good use of class time and can be good speaking tasks in themselves. This is known as "task recycling." This may be as simple as having students change partners after completing a pair-work activity. If the questions in the pair work are interesting, getting answers from a different partner will make it a whole new task. Research shows the benefits of recycling. Lynch and Maclean (2000), for example, showed how requiring students to explain a poster multiple times, to different peers each time, led to gains in accuracy, fluency, and complexity. The least advanced student's explanation became more accurate and more fluent. The most advanced student's explanation became more complex and more precise.

These ideas can be expanded to provide a clear, coherent syllabus for a listening class. A listening class needs a warm-up stage to activate students' prior knowledge. Once the listening tasks have been completed, if time allows, speaking tasks using the same topic (as well as the same vocabulary and structures) can be done in pairs or groups to give practice in interpersonal (face-to-face) listening. Within each speaking task, ideas about planning and recycling language can be applied.

In conclusion, teachers can build on listening tasks to provide speaking practice. At the same time, speaking tasks give students practice in listening to each other.

References and Further Reading

The following books and articles are recommended if you want to learn more about listening or the other topics that have been discussed.

Buck, Gary. *Assessing Listening*. Cambridge: Cambridge University Press, 2001.

* Dörnyei, Zoltán. *The Psychology of the Language Learner: Individual Differences in Second Language Acquisition*. Mahwah, NJ: Lawrence Erlbaum Associates, 2005.

* Ellis, Rod. *Task-based Language Learning and Teaching*. Oxford: Oxford University, Press, 2003.

* Ellis, Rod, ed. *Planning and Task Performance in a Second Language*. Amsterdam: John Benjamins, 2005.

Helgesen, Marc and Steven Brown. *Practical English Language Teaching: Listening*. New York: McGraw-Hill, 2007.

* Lund, Randall J. "A comparison of second language listening and reading." *Modern Language Journal 75* (1991) 196-204, 1991.

* Lynch, Tony and Joan Maclean. "Exploring the benefits of task repetition and recycling for classroom language learning." *Language Teaching Research 4* (2000): 221–250.

* O'Malley, J. and A. Chamot. *Learning Strategies in Second Language Acquisition*. Cambridge: Cambridge University Press, 1990.

* *indicates in-text references*

References and Further Reading

The following books and articles are recommended if you want to learn more about listening or the other topics that have been discussed.

Buck, Gary. *Assessing Listening*. Cambridge: Cambridge University Press, 2001.

* Dörnyei, Zoltán. *The Psychology of the Language Learner: Individual Differences in Second Language Acquisition*. Mahwah, NJ: Lawrence Erlbaum Associates, 2005.

* Ellis, Rod. *Task-based Language Learning and Teaching*. Oxford: Oxford University, Press, 2003.

* Ellis, Rod, ed. *Planning and Task Performance in a Second Language*. Amsterdam: John Benjamins, 2005.

Helgesen, Marc and Steven Brown. *Practical English Language Teaching: Listening*. New York: McGraw-Hill, 2007.

* Lund, Randall J. "A comparison of second language listening and reading." *Modern Language Journal 75* (1991) 196-204, 1991.

* Lynch, Tony and Joan Maclean. "Exploring the benefits of task repetition and recycling for classroom language learning." *Language Teaching Research 4* (2000): 221–250.

* O'Malley, J. and A. Chamot. *Learning Strategies in Second Language Acquisition*. Cambridge: Cambridge University Press, 1990.

* *indicates in-text references*